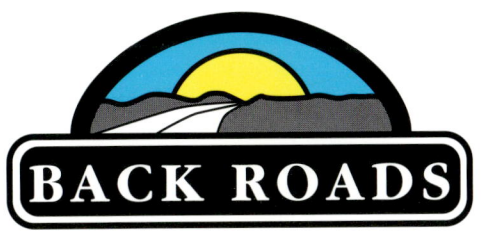

BACK ROADS
PENNSYLVANIA DUTCH COUNTRY

BY LYNN M. STONE

THE ROURKE CORPORATION, INC.
Vero Beach, FL 32964

© 1993 The Rourke Corporation, Inc.

All rights reserved. No part of this book may be reproduced or utilized in any form or by any means, electronic or mechanical including photocopying, recording or by any information storage and retrieval system without permission in writing from the publisher.

Edited by Sandra A. Robinson

PHOTO CREDITS

© Lynn M. Stone: cover, title page, pages 4, 7, 12, 26, 31, 34, 35, 36, 39, 40, 43, 44
© The Pennsylvania Dutch Convention and Visitor's Bureau: pages 9, 11, 14, 42
© Joe McDonald: pages 16, 21, 22, 24, 28
© Mary Ann McDonald: page 19

ACKNOWLEDGEMENTS

The Pennsylvania Dutch Convention and Visitor's Bureau; Steve Scott, the People's Place; Carl and Sally Oman

DEDICATION

For Lynda

Library of Congress Cataloging-in-Publication Data

Stone, Lynn M.
    Pennsylvania Dutch country / by Lynn M. Stone.
        p.   cm. — (Back roads)
    Includes index.
    Summary: An introduction to the geography, history, farming, Amish settlements, and tourist attractions of the Pennsylvania Dutch country.
    ISBN 0-86593-301-4
    1. Pennsylvania Dutch Country (Pa.)—Juvenile literature.
[1. Pennsylvania Dutch Country (Pa.) 2. Pennsylvania—Description and travel. 3. Amish.] I. Title. II. Series: Stone, Lynn M. Back roads.
F157.P44S76   1993
974.8'008'827—dc20
                                                              93-13976
                                                                           CIP
                                                                            AC

Printed in the USA

TABLE OF CONTENTS

1. Pennsylvania Dutch Country 4
2. The Old Pennsylvania Dutch Country 9
3. The Amish 18
4. Amish Community Life 30
5. Pennsylvania Dutch Farms 33
6. Visiting Pennsylvania Dutch Country 38
   Glossary 46
   Index 47

Chapter 1
PENNSYLVANIA DUTCH COUNTRY

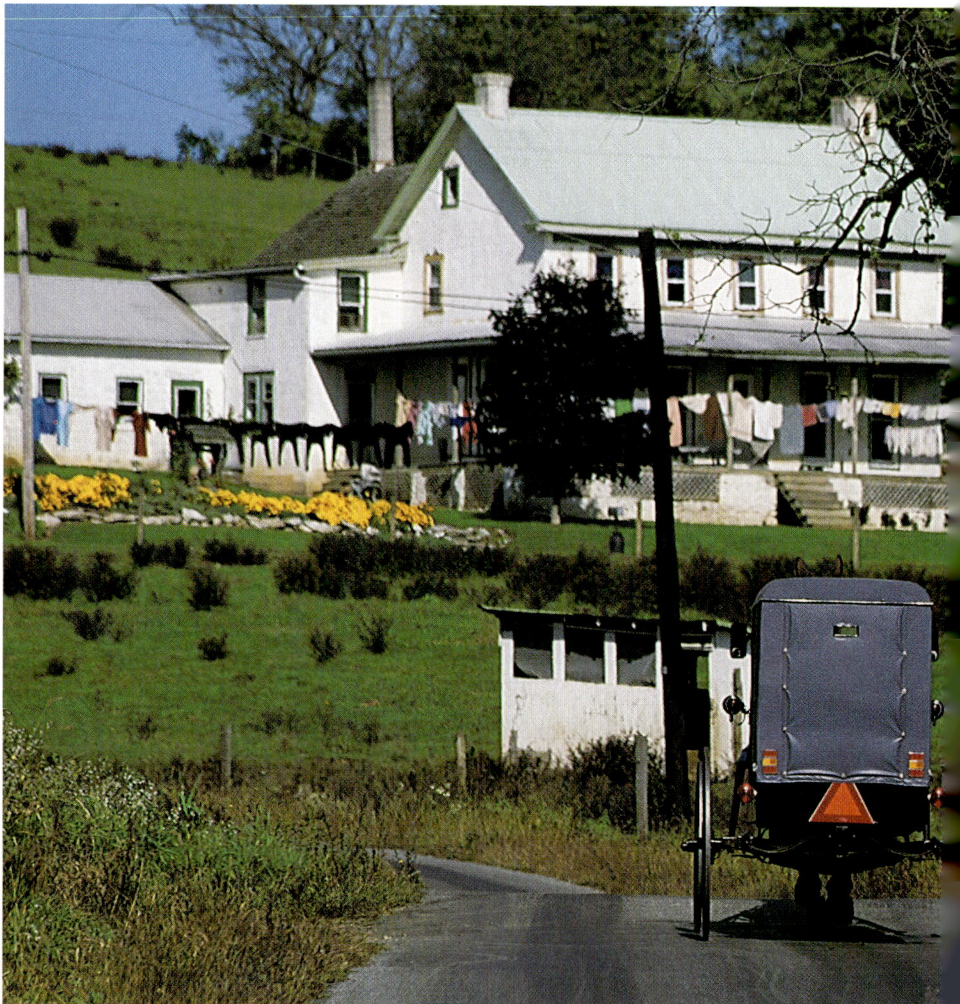

Amish buggies drawn by horses clatter along the back roads of Lancaster County

The many back roads of America are roads to adventure for people who like to "get away." Old back-country roads lead away from busy highways and busy places. Some of them also lead away from the lifestyles of the present and whisk travelers into places where lifestyles of the past linger like morning mist. This is especially true of the back roads that lace Lancaster

County (pronounced LANK uh stir), the heart of Pennsylvania Dutch country. Both automobiles and horse-drawn Amish buggies share the narrow, wandering roads among the hills of Lancaster County.

Rural Lancaster County is especially well-known for its Amish settlements, which have been thriving here for more than 250 years. Many of the Amish people live without electricity and practice the ways of life of their ancestors, such as horse and buggy transport. Although they are closely associated with Lancaster County, the Amish represent a very small percentage of the people in Pennsylvania Dutch country. The Amish who practice the old customs number only 16,000-17,000 of the county's more than 400,000 residents.

In its broadest sense, Pennsylvania Dutch country covers a large chunk of southeastern Pennsylvania. It includes all or parts of 14 counties, a total land area almost the size of New Jersey. Pennsylvania Dutch country stretches east to the Delaware River and south to the Maryland-Pennsylvania state line. On most of the west and north, Pennsylvania Dutch country is bounded by Blue Mountain, the Appalachians' southernmost ridge. This is an area that was settled largely by German **immigrants.** Even today, 300 years after the first German settlers, their influence remains throughout the region. And 3 to 5 million visitors pour into Pennsylvania Dutch country each year for a taste of this unique part of the country. The region's farms and ethnic food, its crafts and historic attractions, are within a one-day's drive of one-quarter of the nation's population. Pennsylvania Dutch country is nearly within the shadow of Philadelphia; and cities such as Boston, New York, Pittsburgh and Washington, D.C., are just hours away.

Fireplaces, clothes drying on the line, and lush gardens reveal Amish reliance upon nature – rather than upon electricity

The term "Pennsylvania Dutch" originated many years ago. Settlers from England and Sweden began to arrive in southeastern Pennsylvania in the late 1600s. They were soon joined by large numbers of Germans and lesser numbers of immigrants from other European countries. In their German language, the German settlers were the *Deutsche* (pronounced DOITCH). But to their English-speaking neighbors, *Deutsche* was generally mispronounced as *Dutch,* and the name stuck.

The Pennsylvania Dutch earned a reputation over the years for fine woodwork, glassware, pottery, pewterware and clocks. They are also known for their productions of Christian music, and their distinctive art. The "hex sign," for example, is a traditional Pennsylvania Dutch design. It usually centers on a colorful variation of a star within a circle. In pioneer days the hex sign was probably displayed to ward off evil spirits. Now the hex signs are simply displayed as traditional art.

The Pennsylvania Dutch also earned a reputation for successful farming. Nowhere is the farming tradition of the Pennsylvania Dutch country more pronounced than in Lancaster County, which is located on part of the Piedmont plateau that lies between the Appalachians and the Atlantic coastal plain. Like an Amish quilt, Lancaster County is a patchwork. Gentle hills mingle with shallow valleys and broad plains. Slow, twisting streams ribbon through the bottomlands. Although 60 percent of Pennsylvania is forested, Lancaster County is mostly open farmland – the most fertile in the state. Lancaster County forests were converted to farmland long ago, and the land has remained largely **agricultural** ever since.

Chapter 2

THE OLD PENNSYLVANIA DUTCH COUNTRY

Hans Herr House and other historic attractions of Pennsylvania Dutch country are within a day's drive for nearly 60 million Americans

Long before the English corrupted *Deutsche* to *Dutch*, the Pennsylvania Dutch country was inhabited by Native Americans. The Delaware, or Lenni-Lenape, lived in the easternmost counties. The Shawnees, an Algonquian tribe, lived in the Susquehanna River valley.

Susquehannocks, also known as Conestogas, lived in Lancaster County. The tribes enjoyed a period of good relations with the first groups of Europeans who moved into southeastern Pennsylvania. But as the number of white homesteaders increased rapidly in the early 1700s, the settlers drove the Native Americans out of southeastern Pennsylvania.

After the first English settlers arrived, the Germans – the Pennsylvania Dutch – began to arrive in large numbers in the late 1600s. German immigration continued well into the 1700s. Most of these people were from the German Rhineland. Some were from German-speaking areas of Switzerland.

The majority of the Pennsylvania Dutch people belonged to either the Lutheran Church or the German Reformed Church. But Mennonites, Amish and Moravians were also among the German-speaking settlers. In Germany and Switzerland, Mennonites and Amish had been persecuted because their religious practices did not conform to the practices of the established churches. Pennsylvania meant new land, opportunity and, most importantly, the freedom of religious expression. Pennsylvania was an ideal refuge for religious minorities because of William Penn, the colony's founder.

William Penn (1644-1718) was born into a family of considerable wealth and status in England. As a young man, he was a bright student. He undoubtedly could have enjoyed a career of influence and wealth in England. But William joined the Quakers, a Christian group known best for its peaceful ways. The official Church of England frowned upon the Quaker movement, just as the

Hex signs grace the peak of a Pennsylvania Dutch building

Most of Lancaster County is gently rolling farmland

established German churches had frowned upon the Mennonites. William's Quaker activities resulted in repeated arrests. He spent eight months in the Tower of London after his first arrest.

William Penn certainly knew first-hand the pain of religious persecution and **intolerance** – the unwillingness

of some people to accept others who have beliefs and customs that are "different." But Penn soon found himself in a position to help religious minorities.

During the reign of Charles II in the mid-1600s, Penn's father had loaned the British government large sums of money. William struck a deal with the government in 1681.

Religious freedom in colonial Pennsylvania prompted members of the radical Ephrata Cloister to settle and construct medieval-style buildings in the old Pennsylvania Dutch country

He agreed to cancel his father's claim against the British treasury in return for wilderness land in eastern North America, most of which the British claimed. The British king could deed huge parcels of new land to almost anyone of rank or influence. Charles II issued a document

that spelled out the boundaries of the land and granted it to William Penn. Already on British records as Sylvania, the land soon became known as Pennsylvania – Penn's Woods – in honor of Admiral Penn, William's father.

William gathered and organized settlers, many of whom were lured by the promise of inexpensive land and freedom. William himself, a gifted writer, authored a **charter** for the government of Pennsylvania. It included a provision for an elected assembly and laws guaranteeing religious freedoms. Penn did not permanently settle in the colony. His thoughtful, democratic ideas of government, however, influenced Pennsylvania law long after his death, and they may have influenced the writers of America's Constitution.

Old Order Amish have continued to follow the customs of their ancestors

Chapter 3

THE AMISH

Because of their unusual customs and dress, both harking back to older times, the Amish people receive much attention from visitors to Pennsylvania Dutch country.

The Amish people are a Christian group. They strive to follow the teachings of Christ in the New Testament of the Bible. They believe in a simple, farm-rooted lifestyle that purposely keeps them somewhat separate from the world at large. The Amish keep themselves apart through a certain amount of **nonconformity** – of not going along with what most people in society do. The strictest Amish groups, often called Old Order Amish, do not have electricity or telephones in their homes, nor do they own automobiles. They dress in plain, **modest** clothes. The men wear beards and broad-brimmed hats. The women wear long dresses. They wear neither makeup nor jewelry. Old Order Amish farmers plow their fields with horses or mules, and milk their cows by hand. They travel by horse and buggy. Naturally, those practices make the Amish the object of great attention by Americans whose lives are closely tied to the automobile and electric

Visitors to the Pennsylvania Dutch country often center their attention on the unusual customs of Amish people

conveniences. Most of that attention is well-meant, but it often results in an uncomfortable loss of privacy for the Amish. They are particularly sensitive about being photographed. The Amish religion forbids their posing for photos, which they consider to be a form of self-centeredness and pride. Many of the Amish, however, graciously let visitors photograph their property.

First-time visitors to Amish farm country in Lancaster County ask: Who are those "plain clothes" people? Why do they cultivate their fields with horse-drawn plows? Why do the women wear long dresses? Why don't they use modern conveniences?

From the Amish point of view, living in the old way is an opportunity to practice the lifestyle that they believe God wants them to follow. The Amish believe they have been called upon to do God's work. That can be done most effectively, they reason, if God's servants separate themselves from worldly influences, such as television, automobiles, higher education and intense competition. The Amish see worldly influences as distractions and temptations that might draw them away from friends, family members, and lives of peace and contentment.

Most of what is necessary and worthwhile, say the Amish, comes from the land. "What better way to remain close to God than through being workers and caretakers of the soil?" they ask. The Old Order Amish and Old Order Mennonites also believe that an **agrarian,** or farming, lifestyle is healthy for the individual and for the family. Farm work keeps the members of a family working together and sharing time together.

Horses and mules still do the plowing for Old Order Amish farmers

Living a simple, farm-rooted lifestyle helps Amish people retain family and community ties, and separate themselves from what they consider the worldliness of society as a whole

The Amish believe that, as Christians, they should be humble and different from world society as a whole. The Old Order Amish express both humility and nonconformity – being different – through their plain, yet distinct dress, and their reliance on horse and buggy for

travel. In another departure from mainstream American society, most Amish and Mennonite groups are **pacifists**. Noting the teachings of Christ, pacifist Amish and Mennonites will not participate in warfare or kill another human being.

Amish youngsters find time away from chores to cycle

Old Order Amish families, usually 30 or 40 of them, make up Amish church districts, or congregations. The congregation is the centerpiece of Amish society. Members are dependent upon each other for fellowship, spiritual support and labor, and in other aspects of their

lives. The congregations do not have churches in the conventional sense. Rather, congregations meet every other week at a member's home for religious services, congregational announcements, dinner and visiting.

A one-room Amish school, where reading, writing and arithmetic are the core of studies

Although known for its Amish settlements, Lancaster County has a much larger population of Mennonites. The Mennonites and Amish are often confused, but they are separate groups. They do share a historical bond, however, and many of the same Christian beliefs. The

essential difference between the groups is in their choice of lifestyles. Mennonite groups tend to be much more "worldly" and mainstream in their lifestyles. Within both the Mennonite and Amish fellowships, though, are several variations. They do not all practice the same codes

Old Order Amish rely on horse and buggy for transport to church services and socials that are held at the homes of members of the congregation

of dress and behavior. Old Order Mennonites, for example, ride in horse-drawn buggies and, like the Amish, avoid higher education. Most "modern" Mennonites do not work on farms, and they embrace higher education enthusiastically.

The roots of the Amish and Mennonites reach back to the Anabaptist Christians of 16th-century Europe. Even then, long before the "modern age," the Anabaptists sought a simple, nonconforming lifestyle that would be similar to that of the earliest Christians. The Anabaptists were persecuted for their customs by both the long-established

Roman Catholic Church and the newly-established Protestant churches in Germany. The Anabaptists might have failed altogether had not Menlo Simons, a former Roman Catholic priest, joined the movement. Simons gathered the scattered Anabaptists, who soon became known as Mennonites, and reorganized them.

The Amish movement began in 1693. Jacob Amman, himself a Swiss Mennonite, felt that his church had weakened its original principles. Along with his followers, soon to be known as the Amish, Amman began a new group separate from the Mennonites.

The first Amish reached Pennsylvania in the early 1700s and set up housekeeping in Berks, Chester and Lancaster counties. Mennonites had already settled in Pennsylvania, establishing Germantown in 1693 near Philadelphia.

Chapter 4

AMISH COMMUNITY LIFE

"Hold fast that which is good" expresses a basic Amish principle. For most of the Amish, the agrarian way of life has been good – satisfying spiritually and physically – since the early days. Of course, it is not a lifestyle for everyone. Some – young people especially – leave the Old Order groups; no one has to stay. But most people who grow up in an Old Order Amish congregation remain. Gradually, the number of Old Order families is growing.

A person does not have to be born into an Amish family to become a member. Unlike many Christian groups, the Amish generally do not recruit members, but they do accept people who demonstrate the will to join the Amish fellowship.

Growing up Amish is not at all like growing up in mainstream America. Amish children are **bilingual.** They learn the traditional German language at home and English in school. Because of the role of German in Amish society, the Amish speak English in a distinct **dialect.**

Amish children attend one-room schools, just as their ancestors and many other Americans of past generations did. School continues only through eighth grade, since the Amish do not approve of formal education beyond that point. Respecting and protecting Amish religious

As Lancaster County farms become more expensive and less available, many Amish families look elsewhere for farmland

rights, the U.S. Supreme Court ruled in 1972 that Amish children did not have to attend school through age 16. Most Amish children have finished eighth grade by the time they are 14. They have a sound background in reading, writing and arithmetic. Science and literature are not a major part of their studies. If Amish children are slighted in the arts and sciences, however, they are well-versed in many of the practical skills that they need as adults in Amish society – soil, plant and animal care, food preservation, carpentry and masonry.

Amish people are usually serious and industrious. Hard work is necessary for the Amish, but it is also part of their tradition. Some say the Amish begin to feel guilty if they are having too much fun. Amish children begin regular chores at an early age. And for the majority of Amish, who work on farms, the work never stops. Nevertheless, Amish youngsters, like children everywhere, find time to skate, sled, play basketball and baseball, bicycle and play with toys, many of them homemade.

On an early October morning, the sun rises over wet pastures, cattle and corn

Although the Amish live somewhat apart from mainstream America, they are not blind to the world around them. They read newspapers, visit doctors and have business dealings with non-Amish. Amish farmers sell their products to tourists and commercial food processors. The Amish frown upon the accumulation of money for the sole purpose of becoming wealthy, but they feel it is important for a family to have enough money to buy farms for its sons as they become adults. In Lancaster County, however, farms are becoming more expensive and less available, forcing many Amish to live elsewhere.

CHAPTER 5

PENNSYLVANIA DUTCH FARMS

On a foggy, dew-soaked dawn in early October, the Pennsylvania Dutch countryside of Lancaster County is an enchanted kingdom. Jeweled beads of moisture cling to shafts of corn and glisten in the still-green tangles of grass that Holstein cattle munch in the gray light. Here and there, in the distance, cattle talk back and forth. A rooster's crow coaxes the perfectly round, Popsicle-orange sun over the next hill. For a moment the fog rises, too, and swallows the sun. In another moment, the sun slips above the wavering fog, now in retreat. Spider webs in the meadows lose their droplets. The last dragonflies of summer, warmed now, flex their wings. The sharp clippety-clop of a horse-drawn buggy tatoos the blacktop. The hum of distant auto traffic grows louder. As the curtain of fog vanishes, barns appear, white castles for cattle and corn. A new day begins in the kingdom.

Farming is a grand tradition in Pennsylvania Dutch country. The real charm of the region is the farm country, some of the oldest farmland in the United States. Early German settlers brought their farming skills, and southeastern Pennsylvania was an ideal workplace. The region had some of the most fertile soil in the nation. Three hundred years later, the farming tradition continues.

Family farming is an old tradition in Pennsylvania Dutch country

Pennsylvania Dutch farms generate 55 percent of the total revenue from Pennsylvania farm products. Lancaster County alone produces 20 percent of the state's total. In addition to dairy products, the Pennsylvania Dutch country produces wheat, corn, tobacco, and a variety of vegetables and fruits, like apples and peaches. Lancaster County is Pennsylvania's breadbasket and dairy mart. In fact, with approximately 95,000 dairy cattle, Lancaster County has more milking cows than all but five other counties in the nation.

In rural Lancaster County, the center of Pennsylvania Dutch farm country, new farming methods coexist with the old. Some farms have the latest, most powerful machinery – tractors that would frighten Godzilla. The Old Order Amish farms, most of them a compact 60 acres or so, have traditional teams of Belgian horses, or other work **breeds.** Some farms employ a combination of old and new methods. But whether a Lancaster County farm operates in the new way or the old, it is likely to be a profitable operation. Many of the modern-day Pennsylvania Dutch are descendants of several generations of farmers. They have fine land and the skills to make the farms produce. Nature cooperates – with well-spaced precipitation averaging 40 to 45 inches per year, and 200 growing days each year.

Only five counties in the nation boast more dairy cattle than Lancaster County's 95,000 head

Belgian horses in Pennsylvania Dutch country are used for more than show

For the Old Order Amish and Mennonites, the family farm provides nearly all of their food. Without electric freezers and refrigerators, Old Order farmers preserve and cure meat. By canning and bottling vegetables and fruits, they keep a supply available throughout the cold months.

The value of farmland in southeastern Pennsylvania is increasing as the amount of farmland decreases. A growing population and its need for support services – homes, shopping centers, highways – takes a toll on farmland. Meanwhile, several organizations in and around Lancaster County are searching for ways to slow the growth of **suburbia** and save the farmland.

Chapter 6

VISITING PENNSYLVANIA DUTCH COUNTRY

Most of the hundreds of thousands who visit the Pennsylvania Dutch country arrive between Memorial Day and Labor Day. Shoppers hunt for the traditional wares of the Pennsylvania Dutch and browse through abundant antique stores. Some of the largest antique clusters are in the New Hope-Lahoska area, New Oxford, Gettysburg and Carlisle.

Festivals and fairs lure thousands of people, too. Just a few among them are the Kutztown Folk Festival, Musikfest in Bethlehem, and Hershey's Fall Meet of the Antique Auto Club. Lancaster County sponsors the Quilters Heritage Celebration, Rhubarb Festival, Outdoor Woodcarving Show, Harvest Festival, Family Oktoberfest and other events.

The region draws history **buffs** from all over North America. More than 700 sites and 90 districts – neighborhoods, for example – of the Pennsylvania Dutch country are recorded in the National Register of Historic Places. Many of these sites are homes or churches. Some are noted for their age or architecture. Some are associated with great people and events. Walking tours are popular in several of the historic districts, including those in Lancaster, Lititz, New Hope and York.

The farm character of Lancaster County is increasingly threatened by suburbia and commercial growth

Sooner or later, tourists make a special point to visit Lancaster County. The Pennsylvania Dutch Convention and Visitor's Bureau is a worthwhile place to begin. Some of Lancaster County's treasures include the old court house (1852); St. James Episcopal Church (1744); President James Buchanan's home (1828); and the Rock Ford Plantation (1792), built by General George Washington's assistant, General Edward Hand. One of the most fascinating historic **relics** of Lancaster County is the Ephrata Cloister. This religious commune was established by Conrad Beissel in 1732. Twenty buildings, most of them originals, still stand nearly two centuries after Beissel's group disbanded. The Hans Herr House (1719), the four-and-one-half story Sickman's Mill, Wright's Ferry Mansion (1738) and the Pennsylvania Farm Museum in Neffsville are also noteworthy.

Fresh produce beckons to autumn visitors in Pennsylvania Dutch country

Most of the Amish farms are in eastern Lancaster County, south of the Pennsylvania Turnpike (I-76), along the back roads that snake beyond Intercourse, Bird-in-Hand, Kinzers, Strasburg and several other towns. Back roads throughout Pennsylvania Dutch country are one of the region's primary attractions. Several of them travel under covered bridges – the region claims more than 60 – and past old mills.

Covered bridges are a specialty of the region. Among the 13 Pennsylvania Dutch counties, nine have covered bridges of historic value. Lancaster County has 22. Bucks and Chester County each has 11. The region's count would be higher, but several covered bridges in Pennsylvania Dutch country have been destroyed by fires and floods. The rain-swollen streams produced by Hurricane Agnes in 1972 were particularly destructive to covered bridges.

Pennsylvania Dutch Country

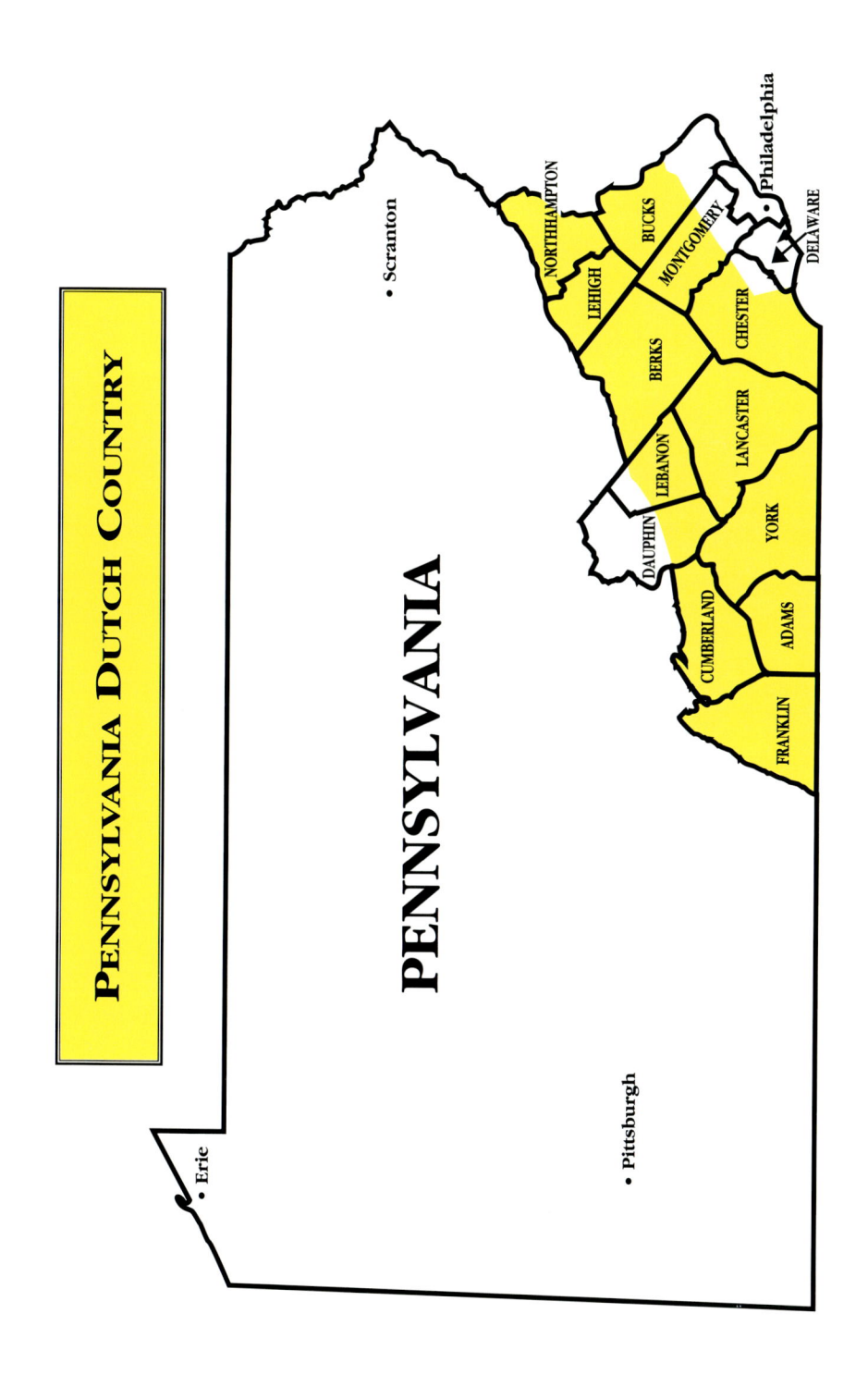

President James Buchanan's home, Wheatland, is one of nearly countless historical attractions in Pennsylvania Dutch country

Some people argue that the Pennsylvania Dutch country's greatest attraction is its food. One popular source of food is the farmer's market. The region has many of them. Local farmers sell their produce, in season, at the markets – sometimes in markethouses more than 100 years old. The tradition of Pennsylvania Dutch farmers hauling products to town is 200 years old.

Restaurants featuring Pennsylvania Dutch cooking abound in the region. Pennsylvania Dutch recipes produce many delicious, but often fattening, dishes. Fried and cured meats are a basic part of the traditional Pennsylvania Dutch menu. Rich, tasty desserts are also standard fare. People on low-fat diets should beware.

Many dishes are unique to the region. *Schnitz un Knepp* is a traditional German feast of dried apples and dumplings. Other regional dishes include pickled pigs' feet (*tzitterle*), hexel and mummix (a type of hash), hog maw (pig stomach stuffed with ground meat and vegetables), apple butter, mush and **scrapple.**

Sooner or later, rural Lancaster County and its Amish farms are on the must-see lists of Pennsylvania Dutch country visitors

The exploration of back roads is a favorite pastime of visitors in Pennsylvania Dutch country

    Many visitors tour the Pennsylvania Dutch country on bicycles. The Pennsylvania Department of Transportation in Harrisburg publishes an excellent introduction to bicycling in Pennsylvania, *The Pennsylvania Bicycling Guide.* The guide's map of southeastern Pennsylvania contains routes, the names of local bike clubs and campground sites. It also lists youth hostels where bicyclists can stay overnight inexpensively, and meet other young bikers and hikers.

Whether a visitor in Pennsylvania Dutch country has an appetite for food, the beauty of traditional farms, or the relics of 300 years of American history, he or she won't leave hungry.

Glossary

agrarian – relating to the farmer's way of life

agricultural – of or relating to farming

bilingual – able to use two languages

breed – a particular type of domestic animal with characteristics that separate it clearly from other animals of the same kind (*Holstein* cattle as separate from *Guernsey* cattle)

buff – a fan or enthusiast

charter – a written contract, deed or constitution

dialect – a regional variation of language distinguished by its vocabulary, pronunciation and use of grammar

immigrant – a person who comes to a country to become a permanent resident

intolerance – the unwillingness to grant equal freedom of expression, especially in religion

modest – that which is decent, plain

nonconformity – refusal to go along with an established church, rule or practice

pacifist – one who is strongly opposed to conflict and war

relic – a trace of the past

scrapple – a mixture of ground meat and cornmeal set in a mold, and served sliced and fried

suburbia – the outlying areas of a town

INDEX

Amish 6, 10, 18, 20, 22, 23, 26, 27, 28, 29, 30, 31, 32, 40
  Old Order 18, 20, 22, 24, 30, 36
Amish settlements 6
Amman, Jacob 29
Anabaptists 28, 29
Appalachians 6, 8
antique stores 38
art 8
Atlantic coastal plain 8
automobiles 6, 18
Beissel, Conrad 39
Berks County, PA 29
Bible 18
bicycling 44
Blue Mountain 6
buggies 6, 18, 22, 28, 33
cattle 18, 33, 34
Charles II, King of England 13, 14
Chester County, PA 29
children, Amish 30, 31
Christ 18, 23
Christians 18, 22, 26, 28, 30
church district (see *congregation*)
churches 25, 29, 38
Church of England 10
congregation 24, 25, 30
Conestogas (see *Susquehannocks*)
covered bridges 40
cows (see *cattle*)
crafts 6
customs 6
Delaware (see *Lenni-Lanape*)
Delaware River 6
dishes (see *food*)
electricity 6, 18
England 10
English language 30
Ephrata Cloister 39
Europe 28
Europeans 10

fairs 38
farmers 18, 32, 35, 36, 42
farmer's market 42
farming 8, 33, 34
farmland 8, 33, 37
farms 6, 28, 31, 33, 34, 35, 36, 40, 45
festivals 38
food 6, 36, 42, 43, 45
German immigration 10
German language 30
German Reformed Church 10
German settlers 6, 8, 33
Germantown, PA 29
Germany 10, 29
Hand, General Edward 39
Hans Herr House 39
hex sign 8
horses 18, 22, 35
hostel, youth 45
Lancaster County, PA 5, 6, 8, 10, 20, 26, 29, 32, 33, 34, 35, 37, 39, 40
Lenni-Lenape 9
Lutheran Church 10
Mennonites 10, 12, 23, 26, 27, 28, 29, 36
  Old Order 20, 28
  Swiss 29
mills 40
Moravians 10
mules 18
National Register of Historic Places 38
Native Americans 9, 10
New Testament 18
pacifists 23
Penn, Admiral 15
Penn, William 10, 12, 13, 15, 17
Pennsylvania 6, 8, 10, 15, 17, 29, 33, 34, 37

INDEX

Pennsylvania Bicycling Guide, The 44
Pennsylvania Department of Transportation 44
Pennsylvania Dutch 8, 10, 33, 35, 38, 43
Pennsylvania Dutch Convention and Visitors Bureau 39
Pennsylvania Farm Museum 39
Pennsylvania Turnpike 40
Philadelphia, PA 6, 29
photos 20
Piedmont plateau 8
"plain clothes" people 20
precipitation 35
Quakers 10, 12
restaurants 43
River, Susquehanna 9
Rock Ford Plantation 39
Roman Catholic Church 29
St. James Episcopal Church 39
schools 30, 31
scrapple 43
Shawnees 9
Sickman's Mill 39
Simons, Menlo 29
suburbia 37
Susquehannocks 10
Switzerland 10
U.S. Supreme Court 31
Wright's Ferry Mansion 39